UTAH JAZZ

ALL-TIME GREATS

BY TED COLEMAN

Book design by Jake Slavik
Cover design by Jake Slavik

Photographs ©: Alex Goodlett/AP Images, cover (top), 1 (top); Douglas C. Pizac/AP Images, cover (bottom), 1 (bottom), 16; Lodriguss/AP Images, 4; Richard J. Carson/AP Images, 6, 8; Ron Schwane/AP Images, 10; Steve C. Wilson/AP Images, 13; Jeremy Harmon/Deseret Morning News/AP Images, 14; Darron Cummings/AP Images, 19; Matt Patterson/AP Images, 20

Press Box Books, an imprint of Press Room Editions.

ISBN
978-1-63494-606-3 (library bound)
978-1-63494-624-7 (paperback)
978-1-63494-642-1 (epub)
978-1-63494-658-2 (hosted ebook)

Library of Congress Control Number: 2022913244

Distributed by North Star Editions, Inc.
2297 Waters Drive
Mendota Heights, MN 55120
www.northstareditions.com

Printed in the United States of America
Mankato, MN
012023

ABOUT THE AUTHOR

Ted Coleman is a freelance sportswriter and children's book author who lives in Louisville, Kentucky, with his trusty Affenpinscher, Chloe.

TABLE OF CONTENTS

MARAVICH
7
JAZZ
7

CHAPTER 1
NOLA TO UTAH

New Orleans, Louisiana, is considered the birthplace of jazz music. It was also the birthplace of the Jazz basketball team. The Jazz began playing in 1974. But first they made a big splash in trading for guard **Pete Maravich**.

"Pistol Pete" was already a star in the NBA. Fans loved his exciting style of play. He was a skilled ball handler. And he could score from anywhere. Maravich made three All-Star Games with the Jazz. However, he couldn't lead New Orleans to a winning record.

DANTLEY
4
Rockets
JAZZ
4
UTAH
JAZZ
35

The team moved to Salt Lake City in 1979. That was the last Jazz season for Maravich. But it was the first for **Adrian Dantley**. The forward was an All-Star right away. He went on to make five more All-Star Games. And he led the league in scoring twice.

Dantley's point guard was **Rickey Green**. The two were great partners. Green played tough defense. In 1983–84, he led the league with 2.7 steals per game. But he was a smart playmaker too. Green knew how to set up stars like Dantley and **Darrell Griffith** to score.

Griffith was a high-flying dunk artist. He and Dantley were true scoring machines. The Jazz

STAT SPOTLIGHT

CAREER POINTS PER GAME

JAZZ TEAM RECORD

Adrian Dantley: 29.6

became one of the top scoring teams in the NBA.

The team's center for much of the 1980s was **Mark Eaton.** Eaton was a defensive force. He set the Jazz record for blocks his rookie year. He broke his own record six more times.

When in need, the Jazz could count on **Thurl Bailey**. The forward came off the bench more than he started. But he did a lot with his limited playing time. Bailey was a team captain and a steady scorer.

The Jazz improved a lot in the early 1980s. They had their first winning record in 1983–84. But there was plenty more to come. The Jazz's greatest ever players were soon arriving.

COACH LAYDEN

Frank Layden worked for the Jazz for 20 years. He was general manager from 1979 to 1987. From 1981 to 1988 he also served as head coach. He took the Jazz to the playoffs for the first time. Layden then became team president until 1999. Layden was responsible for building the greatest Jazz teams in history.

STOCKTON
12
JAZZ
12
SPALDING
NBA

CHAPTER 2
NBA FINALISTS

The Jazz had a solid core of good players during the early 1980s. It got even better in 1984. Utah picked point guard **John Stockton** in the draft. Stockton was not a stylish player. He was just great at everything he did.

Stockton worked hard. He could shoot. He could play defense. And he created tons of chances for his teammates. Stockton had more assists and steals than anyone in NBA history.

The Jazz had good luck in the 1985 draft, too. The team chose power forward

STAT SPOTLIGHT

CAREER ASSISTS

NBA RECORD

John Stockton: 15,806

Karl Malone. Malone stood 6'9" tall. And he weighed more than 250 pounds. That made him a powerful force to defend.

Malone was nicknamed "The Mailman." That was because he always delivered on the court. Only two players in NBA history had more points than Malone.

Malone and Stockton became one of the league's best duos. Guard **Jeff Hornacek**'s arrival in 1994 gave Utah a "big three." Hornacek could light it up from three-point range. As the third scoring option, he made the team even tougher to beat.

JAZZ
32
MALONE
32

TAYLOR
2
JAZZ
00
OSTERTAG
00

Greg Ostertag did not score much. But the center was a strength under the basket defensively. In the 1996–97 season the Jazz set a team record with 64 wins. When Ostertag was on the floor they regularly outscored their opponents.

The Jazz made the NBA Finals for the first time in 1997. They made it again in 1998. But both times they lost to the Chicago Bulls. That was the high point of the Stockton-Malone era. Stockton and Malone were gone by 2003–04. But the players of this era remain favorites among Jazz fans.

COACH SLOAN

Jerry Sloan was a Jazz assistant coach in the 1980s. He took over as head coach in 1988. He held the job for 23 years. Sloan was by far the team's most successful coach. He took the team to two NBA Finals. Few coaches in NBA history stuck around as long as Sloan. He is one of just five to have 1,200 career wins.

KIRILENKO
47
JAZZ
47

CHAPTER 3

SWEET MUSIC

It's never easy to replace legendary players. **Andrei Kirilenko** proved to be a worthy next star. The forward had a variety of skills. He could score lots of points. And he was named to the All-Defensive Team three times.

Center **Mehmet Okur** excelled on both ends of the court, too. Centers often play under the basket. Okur could also score from outside. He retired fourth in Jazz history for three-pointers.

Running this Jazz offense was point guard **Deron Williams**. Williams was a speedy player. That burst helped him make plays for his teammates. He made plenty of baskets himself, though. Williams averaged more than 18 points per game five times in Utah.

A veteran presence on the team was **Carlos Boozer**. The forward was intense and hard to stop. That included both offense and defense. He averaged a double-double in his time with Utah.

Forward **Paul Millsap** was a late draft pick in 2006. But he worked his way into the lineup. Millsap became better the more he

HOT ROD

Rodney "Hot Rod" Hundley was with the Jazz from the beginning. The former player was hired as the Jazz's broadcaster for their first season. He followed the team to Utah. He held his job until retiring in 2009. Hundley called more than 3,000 Jazz games over 35 years. A banner honoring him hangs alongside those of great Jazz players at Utah's home arena.

played. And he rarely missed a game in Utah.

Forward **Gordon Hayward** was a top-10 draft pick in 2010. It took some time for him to settle into the NBA. Eventually he grew into an All-Star. By 2016–17 he was averaging nearly 22 points per game.

By then the Jazz had a new star. **Rudy Gobert** was a defensive machine.

MITCHELL
45

The towering center won his first Defensive Player of the Year award in 2018. He won again in 2019 and 2021.

His combination with guard **Donovan Mitchell** helped Utah win a lot of games. Mitchell was a very athletic player. And he could score from anywhere. Mitchell averaged 20 points per game his first five years in the NBA. In 2022, the Jazz traded Gobert. They believed Mitchell was the player who could lead them back to the Finals.

STAT SPOTLIGHT

THREE-POINTERS IN A SEASON

JAZZ TEAM RECORD

Donovan Mitchell: 232 (2021-22)

TIMELINE

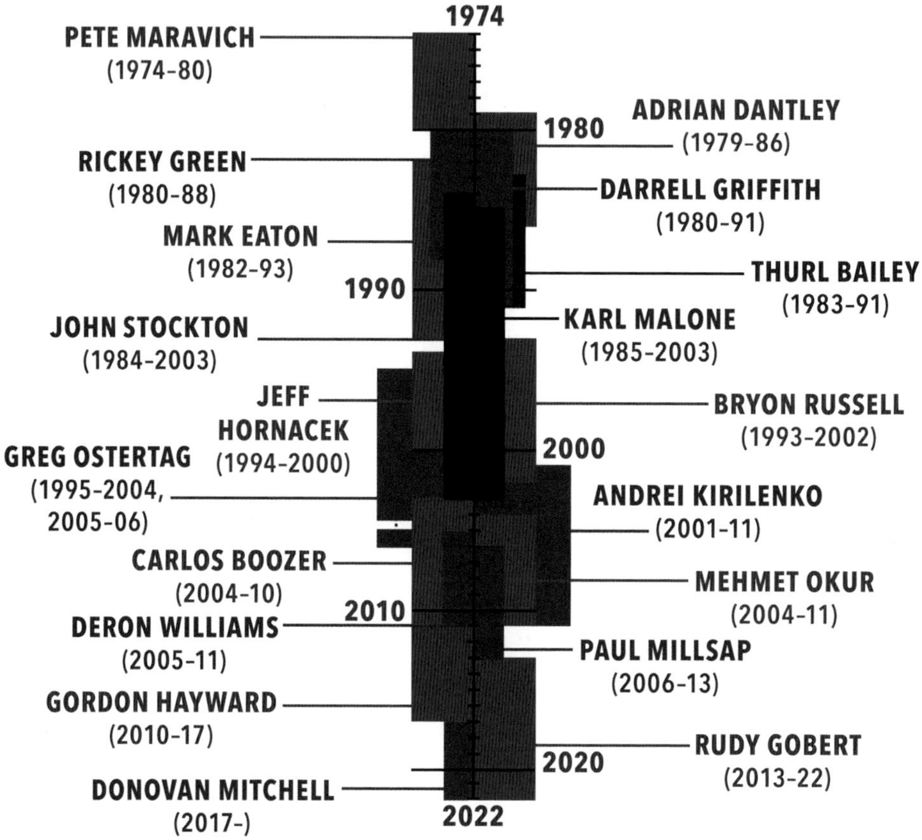
1974
PETE MARAVICH (1974-80)
1980
ADRIAN DANTLEY (1979-86)
RICKEY GREEN (1980-88)
DARRELL GRIFFITH (1980-91)
MARK EATON (1982-93)
THURL BAILEY (1983-91)
1990
JOHN STOCKTON (1984-2003)
KARL MALONE (1985-2003)
JEFF HORNACEK (1994-2000)
BRYON RUSSELL (1993-2002)
GREG OSTERTAG (1995-2004, 2005-06)
2000
ANDREI KIRILENKO (2001-11)
CARLOS BOOZER (2004-10)
MEHMET OKUR (2004-11)
2010
DERON WILLIAMS (2005-11)
PAUL MILLSAP (2006-13)
GORDON HAYWARD (2010-17)
RUDY GOBERT (2013-22)
2020
DONOVAN MITCHELL (2017-)
2022

TEAM FACTS

UTAH JAZZ

Formerly: New Orleans Jazz (1974–75 to 1979–80)

First season: 1974–75

NBA championships: 0*

Key coaches:

Frank Layden (1981–82 to 1988)
277–294, 18–23 playoffs

Jerry Sloan (1988–89 to 2010–11)
1,127–682, 96–100 playoffs

MORE INFORMATION

To learn more about the Utah Jazz, go to **pressboxbooks.com/AllAccess.**

These links are routinely monitored and updated to provide the most current information available.

**Through 2021–22 season*

GLOSSARY

assists
Passes that lead directly to baskets.

captain
A team's leader.

double-double
Accumulating 10 or more of two certain statistics in a game.

draft
A system that allows teams to acquire new players coming into a league.

era
A period of time in history.

general manager
The person in charge of a sports team, whose duties include signing and trading players.

intense
Extremely earnest or serious.

rookie
A first-year player.

veteran
A player who has spent several years in a league.

INDEX